FOREST ANIMALS

Explore the Fascinating Worlds of . . .

BLACK BEARS
by Kathy Feeney

MOOSE
by Anthony D. Fredericks

WHITETAIL DEER
by Laura Evert

WOLVES
by Laura Evert

Illustrations by John F. McGee

NORTHWORD
Minnetonka, Minnesota

Photography © 2000: Erwin & Peggy Bauer: pp. 137, 150-151, 184; Craig Brandt: cover-moose, pp. 52, 60-61, 91, 156-157; Robin Brandt: pp. 62, 68-69, 75, 153; John R. Ford: pp. 98, 128-129; Michael H. Francis: pp. 7, 14, 36, 44-45, 46, 55, 56-57, 65, 76, 84, 85, 92, 109, 110-111, 138-139, 146-147, 160, 165, 169, 170-171, 173, 182, 183; Howie Garber/www.wanderlustimages.com: pp. 22-23, 67, 142, 178-179, 180; Rita Groszmann: cover-wolf, pp. 4, 18, 25, 32-33, 37, 42-43, 144, 154, 162-163, 176; Lisa & Mike Husar/Team Husar: pp. 34-35, 82-83, 87, 113, 174-175; Donald M. Jones: cover-black bear, pp. 6, 8-9, 12-13, 30, 53, 58, 78-79, 122; Bill Lea: cover-whitetail deer, pp. 10, 17, 19, 20-21, 28-29, 39, 41, 102, 106-107, 116-117, 119, 120, 124, 132-133, 134; Tom & Pat Leeson: pp. 50, 88, 148, 159, 166-167; Robert McCaw: pp. 27, 66, 130; David A. Murray: pp. 72-73; Mark Raycroft: pp. 38, 96, 100-101, 103, 104, 114, 145; Mark Wallner/Wing It Wildlife: pp. 70, 99.

Illustrations by John F. McGee

NorthWord Books For Young Readers
11571 K-Tel Drive
Minnetonka, MN 55343
www.tnkidsbooks.com

Library of Congress Cataloging-in-Publication Data

Forest animals / illustrations by John F. McGee.
    p. cm.
    Four works originally published independently. 2000, in series: Our wild world series. Contents: Black bears / by Kathy Feeney – Moose / by Anthony D. Fredericks – Whitetail deer ; Wolves / by Laura Evert.
    ISBN 1-55971-708-4 (hardcover)
    1. Forest animals – Juvenile literature. 2. Black bear – Juvenile literature. 3. Moose – Juvenile literature. 4. White-tailed deer – Juvenile literature. 5. Wolves – Juvenile literature. [1. Forest animals.] I. McGee, John F., ill.

QL112.F68 2000
591.73–dc21
                                                    00-064312
Printed in Malaysia

10 9 8 7 6 5 4

FOREST ANIMALS

TABLE OF CONTENTS

Explore the Fascinating World of . . .

Black Bears

Kathy Feeney
Illustrations by John F. McGee

SOME PEOPLE fear the mighty black bear. They know bears are extremely strong, with sharp claws and dangerous teeth. But most black bears are actually shy and solitary mammals. They avoid contact with people and even other bears. They prefer to be left alone!

There are eight species (SPEE-sees), or kinds, of bear. They are the North American black bear, the Asiatic black bear, the brown (or grizzly) bear, the giant panda, the polar bear, the sloth bear, the spectacled bear, and the sun bear.

They all may belong to the same family, but there are many differences between these bear types. They live in different parts of the world. For example, the spectacled bear is found in South America and the Asiatic black bear lives in Asia. They are also different in size. The brown bear is very large and the sun bear is quite small. Most bears move quickly but the sloth bear moves very slowly.

Even the large black bear moves quietly in its forest home.

Young bears are only playing when they nip at each other.

Another difference may be their coat colors. But no matter what color a bear's coat is, it works like camouflage (KAM-uh-flaj). It protects the bear by helping it blend into its natural habitat. This helps it hide from predators, or enemies.

Polar bears, for example, have yellowish-white fur. They are hard to see in their snowy Arctic surroundings. Giant pandas are both black and white. This color combination helps them blend into the shadowy mountain forests of China.

Black bears are almost always black with tan muzzles, or snouts. They also can be dark brown, cinnamon, or tan. Sometimes they have a white patch of hair on their throat or chest.

North American black bears are the most common bear species in the world today. They live only in North America. Many of their woodland and mountain habitats are also inhabited by humans. This is the kind of bear that people are most likely to see in the wild.

Bears often travel through wide open spaces,
and can quickly "disappear" into nearby trees.

This mother and baby are different colors,
but they are both North American black bears.

The area where a bear lives is called its home range, or territory. The size of the territory depends on the amount of food it has for the bear. If there is little food, a bear needs a larger territory to find enough to eat. It could be as small as 3 square miles (7.8 square kilometers) or as large as 10 square miles (26 square kilometers). A bear usually protects and stays in the same territory its whole life. But bears do not choose one place to live inside this area. They prefer to roam, or wander, throughout their home range. They may sleep in a different place each night.

A young female black bear often chooses her territory near her mother's home range. Young males usually travel far from their mother's territory to find their own home range.

Bears are diurnal (die-YER-nul), meaning they move around during the day and at night. When bears become tired, they stop right where they are to rest. They often make a bed of grass and leaves in the shade. A thicket of bushes makes a safe place for sleeping. A pile of rocks or a cave also provides good hidden shelter. Females with babies, called cubs, often rest near a tree so the young can quickly climb the tree to escape danger.

Black Bears
FUNFACT:

The scientific name for the
North American black bear is
Ursus americanus.

Pages 12-13: A spruce tree provides a safe place for this bear cub to wait for its mother.

Black bears can grow to about 6 feet (1.8 meters) long. They weigh as much as 200 to 600 pounds (91 to 272 kilograms). Some bears have weighed more than 800 pounds (360 kilograms). Males are called boars. They are larger and heavier than females, which are called sows.

A bear's long, thick body is very muscular and athletic under its heavy coat of hair. Its tail is short and stubby. Its head is large. Black bears have small eyes with poorer eyesight than many other animals. But they can distinguish colors and see movement. Bears have small, round ears and their hearing is very good. They can hear many high-pitched sounds that humans cannot hear.

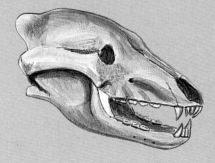

When they stand upright, bears look even bigger and more dangerous.

A bear's sense of smell, with its long snout and black nose, is excellent. Bears usually walk slowly and stop often, lifting their snouts into the air to sniff for food or danger. Scientists estimate that a bear's sense of smell is 15 times greater than a person's sense of smell. Bears can sniff food from more than 3 miles (4.8 kilometers) away. That would be like a person being able to smell cookies baking in a house across town!

Even though black bears have short legs, they can run in bursts up to 30 miles (48 kilometers) per hour. That's as fast as a horse, and much faster than a human.

Bears are also strong swimmers. They do the "dog-paddle" to cross a river, lake, or stream. Bears may use the water to cool off in the warm weather, and as a way to escape predators. When a bear leaves the water, it usually shakes its soaked coat, just like a big wet dog. This removes water and dirt from its fur.

A bear also may lick its coat clean. Sometimes bears roll around in the mud. They do this to get rid of fleas! When bears feel itchy from a fly or an insect bite, they scratch their fur against the bark of a tree. You might be able to tell if a bear has been in the area by looking for clumps of bear hair stuck to the trunk of a tree.

Sometimes people say they are "as hungry as a bear." That's because bears eat so much and so often. In fact, they spend most of their day searching for things to eat.

More than 80 percent of a bear's diet is plants. They often eat berries, fruit, flowers, and many kinds of nuts, including acorns. They also consume grasses, twigs, and roots. But bears are omnivores (OM-ni-vorz), which means they eat both plants and meat. Bears eat many insects and sometimes they eat animals such as mice or squirrels.

Black Bears
FUNFACT:

An adult bear can reach an
apple on a tree branch
7 to 8 feet above the ground.

This black bear's sense of smell probably led it to search for food in this hollow tree stump.

Soapberries make a tasty snack for a hungry bear.

Bears may wade into streams and rivers to catch fish with their feet, or paws. They stick their long, sensitive tongues into tree trunks to catch ants and termites. Bears also eat tree sap. To get sap, they scratch the bark off a tree. Then they lick the tree as the sweet sap oozes from inside. It is the same sap that people collect to make syrup for their pancakes.

People can guess what a bear ate by the color of its droppings, or scat. It may be purplish, for example, after the bear has eaten blueberries.

Scat is usually dark in color and looks like a pile of marbles with some berries in it. If the bear has consumed ripe apples, the scat is lighter and looks mushy. The scat of a bear that has been eating fish has fish scales in it.

You can tell the bear ate cranberries by looking at these droppings.

Bears know that ants and other insects can be found under rocks.

Honey is a favorite food. Bears get their honey fresh from bee nests. These nests are called beehives. When bears find beehives hanging in trees, they climb the tree and scoop the thick, golden honey out of the hive with their big paws. Then they eat the honey and the entire nest, including the bees. The bees often sting the bears but that doesn't keep them from looking for another beehive!

Bears also dig up roots and use their claws to find insects in hollow logs. They even turn over large rocks to find food underneath them.

Black Bears
FUNFACT:

In their strong jaw, bears have 42 teeth, which easily crush, grind, and tear food. Humans have 32 teeth.

Bears are excellent at fishing, and this salmon will make a good meal.

Scientists who study animals are called zoologists (zoe-OL-uh-jists). They have learned that bears have excellent memories. Just as people remember the names of their favorite restaurants, bears remember places where they have found tasty meals. Somehow they remember how to get there and when the food is ready to eat. They often return to the same location year after year. When young bears are shown the routes or trails to these good feeding areas, they begin using them too.

Eating huge amounts of food in the summer and fall is one way black bears prepare for winter. In fact, they overeat on purpose to gain extra weight—often more than 100 pounds (45 kilograms). Bears need a thick layer of fat for warmth and nourishment during the winter.

Another way to prepare for winter is for the bear to grow a thick layer of fur under its softer, lighter summer coat. In the spring, the bear sheds this fur to keep cooler in the warm weather of summer. The top layer is made up of long, shiny hairs called guard hairs.

Black Bears
FUNFACT:

People eat about 1,500 calories each day. In the fall, a bear may consume 15,000 calories each day!

Just before winter, bears look very fat and ready for a long sleep.

By the end of fall, each bear must find a place to sleep through the winter. Bears often use a cave or fallen hollow tree. Bears also dig a hole in the ground. These homes, called dens, provide both shelter and safety until spring.

The size of the den depends on the size of the bear. A bear needs just enough room to turn around inside the den. A larger den would waste precious body heat. Bears usually sleep in a den only one winter. They find a new one each year.

This winter sleep is called hibernation (hi-ber-NAY-shun). Bears hibernate to conserve energy. They do this because vegetation and other food sources are extremely scarce during cold weather, especially if there is snow on the ground.

Most bears do not even eat or drink during their hibernation. Some bears in the warmer areas of North America occasionally leave the den for a short time. Then they go back to hibernating.

During hibernation, a bear's metabolism (meh-TAB-o-liz-um) decreases. This means its heartbeat, blood flow, and breathing are slower. Somehow bears remain healthy and their muscles stay strong until they emerge (ee-MERJ), or come out of the den, in the spring.

There are many mysteries about black bear hibernation that zoologists continue to study.

Deep snow often camouflages the entrance to a bear den.

Bear cubs learn to stay together when their mother is away.

Bears do not usually live together in groups. Even after adults breed in the summer, they go their separate ways. Boars do not stay around to help the sows raise their cubs.

That means when a sow is going to have babies she must find a safe site, or location, for a den by herself. She carefully makes a soft bed with nearby leaves and twigs. She knows that her cubs will be born in about January. This happens while the sow is still hibernating!

Black Bears
FUNFACT:

Bear species are found everywhere in the world except Australia, Africa, and Antarctica.

Most adult bears have few enemies to worry about in their home territory.

Black bears give birth only once every two years. Sows may have as many as four cubs at a time. The group is called a litter. A newborn bear cub is smaller than a squirrel. Each one weighs about 10 ounces (283 grams) and measures about 8 inches (20 centimeters) long.

Bears are born bald and toothless. But they already have claws.

After the mother gives birth, she licks her cubs clean. Bear cubs get nourishment from drinking their mother's milk. They stay warm snuggling against their mother's fur. The mother and her newborns remain together in the den until spring.

By then each cub weighs nearly 8 pounds (4 kilograms). They have tasted only their mother's milk. They are fat, furry, and eager to leave their den.

When adult bears finally emerge in the spring, they are very hungry and thirsty. They have lost weight during hibernation and are ready to eat again!

Cubs learn many important things from their mother, like how to find food.

The mother bear spends this first summer teaching her cubs many things. She shows them how to eat new foods and where to find them.

Cubs learn to carefully watch their mother at all times. If there is danger, she warns them to quickly climb a nearby tree. And she signals to them when it is safe to come down. She often climbs the tree with them to avoid danger on the ground.

Bear cubs are very curious. They are playful and want to discover their new world. If they wander too far away from their mother, she calls them back with grunts.

She may also "woof" like a dog to warn them of predators such as eagles, bobcats, and wolves. Sometimes even adult male bears are dangerous to young bears.

Splashing through a stream keeps these bear cubs
cool in the warm summer sunshine.

When the weather turns cold, the mother bear and her cubs find a new den and spend a second winter together. This time, the cubs hibernate too.

In the spring when these cubs emerge from the den, they are called yearlings. They usually leave their mother for good the following summer.

Bear siblings, or brothers and sisters, sometimes continue to live together after they leave their mother. By a year later, they each go their own way and are completely on their own.

Black Bears
FUNFACT:

The bear is related to the dog, the fox, and the wolf.

Climbing a tree, even a small one, keeps this cub safe from predators.

We may not understand bear "talk," but cubs do!

Some claw marks are deep and easy to see, since a black bear's claws may be 2 inches (5 centimeters) long.

Bears keep in touch by snorting, whining, and making a sound like a roar. Bears can communicate silently in several ways too. When its ears are straight up, a bear is at ease. If they are laid back, the bear is probably angry, especially at a misbehaving cub.

Bears also claw tree trunks. These scratches tell other bears to keep out of their territory.

Sniffing the air is a way for a black bear to know if other bears are in the area. Each bear has its own unique scent (SENT), or odor.

During the breeding season, adult male bears rub their scent on trees to attract a mate. That scent is also in a bear's scat and in its tracks.

This bear may be sniffing the air for trespassers as it marks its territory.

One way for people to know if a bear has been in the area is to see its tracks on the ground. Each black bear paw has five toes and five sharp, curved claws. The back, or hind, tracks usually measure about 4 inches (10 centimeters) wide and 8 inches (20 centimeters) long. The front tracks are smaller.

The end of the track with the claw mark points in the direction that the bear was traveling. If the tracks are close together the bear was probably walking slowly. The farther apart the tracks are, the faster the bear was walking or running.

The black bear's flat and wide paws help it stand upright on its hind legs. Sometimes bears stand straight up to grab food out of trees or to get a better view. The fur and padding on the bottom of the paws help the bear travel quietly.

Black Bears
FUNFACT:

Two star constellations are named for bears: Ursa Major ("Great Bear") and Ursa Minor ("Little Bear"). They also are known as The Big Dipper and The Little Dipper.

Bears often leave a trail with their paw prints,
and you can tell which way they went.

A mother bear may attack if an enemy bothers her cubs.
She guards them well.

Black bears can be dangerous if they are disturbed while eating.

Bears are peaceful by nature. But they may attack if they are surprised. A mother bear will fight off any predators that threaten her cubs.

An angry bear lowers its head and stares at its enemy with its ears flat back. The bear then slaps the ground with its paws and clicks its teeth before charging. Sometimes bears fight standing on their hind legs. When most animals see a bear's enormous body, huge teeth, and sharp claws, they quickly leave!

Black Bears
FUNFACT:

Early pioneers used black bear hair for fishing lures, and to stuff mattresses and pillows. Bear fat was even recommended as a cure for baldness!

Living in good habitat, this cub may live up to twenty-five years.

Zoologists estimate that there are about 500,000 black bears in North America. And the bear populations in some areas of the United States are growing' steadily.

But the loss of good habitat is a threat to bear survival in other areas. When people build houses in the forests where bears live, the bears lose their natural homes and many die.

Our national parks and forests have habitats that will never be destroyed. And bears living there will always have good territories to roam.

Fortunately, there are many people who respect the North American black bear and work very hard to protect its habitat and food sources. This will help the bear survive and continue to live in the wild.

Black Bears
FUNFACT:

Native Americans believed bears were sacred animals. They wore bear-tooth necklaces for good luck.

My FOREST ANIMAL Adventures

The date of my adventure: _____

The people who came with me: _____

_____

Where I went: _____

What forest animals I saw:

_____   _____

_____   _____

_____   _____

_____   _____

The date of my adventure: _____

The people who came with me: _____

_____

Where I went: _____

What forest animals I saw:

_____   _____

_____   _____

_____   _____

_____   _____

My FOREST ANIMAL Adventures

The date of my adventure: _____

The people who came with me: _____

_____

Where I went: _____

What forest animals I saw:

_____   _____

_____   _____

_____   _____

_____   _____

The date of my adventure: _____

The people who came with me: _____

_____

Where I went: _____

What forest animals I saw:

_____   _____

_____   _____

_____   _____

_____   _____

Explore the Fascinating World of . . .

Moose

Anthony D. Fredericks
Illustrations by John F. McGee

WHAT IS THE world's strangest-looking animal? Is it the giraffe with its long neck? Is it the raccoon with its striped tail and black face mask? Or is it the elephant with its long trunk? All those animals certainly are unusual. But many people think the strangest-looking animal is the moose.

At first glance you might think that big mistakes were made with the moose. In fact, some people say that a moose looks as if it had been put together with parts of other animals.

For example, a moose has a short tail like a deer. It has a beard hanging from its chin like a turkey, and big ears like a burro. It has four skinny legs like a horse, large shoulder humps like a bear, and a stomach with four chambers like a cow.

A moose's long nose is sometimes called a snout, or a moose "muffle."

This young moose stays close to its mother, wherever she goes.

Moose have been around for millions of years. They belong to a group of animals called ungulates (UN-gyoo-lutz), because they have hooves. Also in this group are elk, caribou, whitetail deer, and reindeer. They all are even-toed mammals. That means each hoof has two large toes and two small toes. Humans are odd-toed mammals because we have five toes on each foot.

There are seven different types of moose. Four types are found only in North America, two in Asia, and one in Europe. Scientists who study animals are called zoologists (zoe-OL-uh-jists). They have given every known animal a scientific name. The scientific name for moose is *Alces alces* (AL-sees, AL-sees).

Moose
FUNFACT:

A moose's two small toes
are called dew claws.

Moose are usually shy animals, and prefer to stay
hidden in the forest, in winter and summer.

The word "moose" comes from the Algonquin Indians. These were native people who lived throughout the northern regions of Canada. The Algonquins called this strange-looking creature *mooswa*. It means "twig-eater" or "the animal that strips bark off of trees." Early explorers heard this word and through the years, it eventually changed into "moose."

For the Algonquins, the moose was an important animal. It supplied them with food and other things for their survival. Moose meat was a source of nourishment during the long winters. The hide was used to make clothing and provide shelter. And moose bones and antlers were shaped into useful tools.

To find enough food and the right kind of food,
a moose may begin the search very early in the morning.

Even young moose have learned to be on the alert for danger that might be nearby.

When early explorers first came to North America, the moose's range extended as far south as what is now the state of Virginia. Moose proved to be a valuable food source for those early settlers. Unfortunately, as a result, moose were hunted to near extinction along the Atlantic coast.

Today, moose populations are growing, and they can be found throughout every province of Canada and many areas in the United States. These include the states of Idaho, Montana, New Hampshire, North Dakota, Vermont, Wisconsin, and Wyoming. The largest concentrations of moose are in Alaska, Maine, Michigan, and Minnesota.

The area where a moose lives and feeds is called its home range. Zoologists have estimated that a single moose needs about 4 square miles (6.5 square kilometers) of forest or pastureland in order to survive. Some moose have much larger ranges. If there is plenty of food in a particular area, moose stay within that area. If the food supply runs out, they move to other locations to obtain the food they need. It is not unusual for moose to live their whole lives within a 10-mile (16 kilometers) radius.

Moose
FUNFACT:

There are about 80,000 moose in the lower 48 U.S. states, 175,000 in Alaska, and 800,000 in Canada.

Winter can be a difficult time for moose.
But if there is a good supply of food, they will find it.

It is not unusual for older, healthy cows to have twin babies. Sometimes they even have triplets.

Although the moose truly is one of Nature's strangest-looking creatures, its design is well suited for living in its northern habitat.

The first thing you notice about a moose is its large body. It can be as long as 10 feet (3.5 meters). Some moose measure as tall as 7 feet (2.14 meters) at the shoulder.

Female moose are called cows, and may weigh as much as 800 pounds (364 kilograms). Males are called bulls, and may weigh between 900 and 1,800 pounds (410 to 810 kilograms). That would be equal to having about 25 of your friends standing in the same place at the same time!

Moose have very long legs. When you look closely, you'll notice something else very interesting about them. Most four-legged animals have legs that are all the same length. But the moose's front legs are actually longer than its back legs. If a moose takes a drink from the edge of a pond or stream, it may kneel on its front legs to reach the water.

Moose are not jumpers. They prefer to walk around or just step over something in the way. But a moose's long legs allow it to easily walk in very deep snow and wade through ponds and streams. Its long legs keep its belly about 40 inches (103 centimeters) off the ground. You could probably walk right under a moose!

Another feature you'll notice about a moose is its very large nose. It also has a "beard" that hangs from its chin. This flap of skin covered with hair is called a dewlap, or bell. Both bulls and cows have one. Even a baby moose, called a calf, has a very short one. An adult's dewlap is about 8 to 10 inches (20 to 26 centimeters) long. Dewlaps tend to be longer on males than on females.

Zoologists aren't exactly sure about the purpose of the dewlap. Some believe it is used to spread scent, or odor, during mating.

Moose
FUNFACT:

The moose is the largest member of the deer family. Some people know it by its nickname "Old Bucketnose."

The long and thick dewlap helps tell that this is
an older bull in very good health.

To hear better, moose can move one ear at a time.
To see better, they can move one eye at a time.

The coat of a moose is very dark brown. It is made up of hairs called guard hairs, which can measure up to 10 inches (25.4 centimeters) long. And believe it or not, these hairs are hollow. The air trapped inside is warmed by the moose's body heat to insulate it against the cold weather.

The hollow hair also helps the moose float when it swims across a lake or pond.

In the fall, moose grow a layer of thick fur under the guard hairs to help with winter insulation. Each spring, moose shed this layer to be cooler for the summer.

A calf quickly learns to keep up with its mother, on land and in the water.

At first glance a moose seems awkward. But it can run very fast. A moose may need to run to escape predators, or enemies, like black bears, grizzly bears, and wolves.

It is not unusual for a frightened moose to gallop at speeds up to 35 mph (56 kph). That's the average speed limit for cars on many city streets.

Most of the time, however, moose are content to wander peacefully and quietly through their habitat searching for food.

Moose are mostly solitary creatures. They prefer to live and eat by themselves. As a result, moose are rarely found in groups, or herds. When they do get together, it's only because several moose have discovered a good feeding area at the same time. When the food is gone, the moose go off by themselves to find other food sources.

With no predator in sight, this moose should be
able to eat and drink in safety.

Zoologists believe that moose eat water plants because they contain large amounts of sodium, or salt, which the moose needs in its diet.

Some animals migrate, or travel, from one location to another. They do this to breed or look for food. Animals such as caribou and elk are known for traveling long distances. Moose are closely related to these species (SPEE-sees), or kinds, of migrating animals.

But moose do not migrate. It would be safe to say that moose wander rather than migrate. That means they go wherever the food is. In summer they may wander up into the mountains. In fall they may wander down to heavily forested areas. They have no preferred routes or territories—they simply look for the best way to the best feeding areas.

Most people eat many different kinds of food. These may include fruits, vegetables, bread, meat, and fish. Humans are omnivores (OM-ni-vorz) because they eat both plants and meat. Moose, however, are herbivores (HERB-uh-vorz) because they eat only plants.

When moose are in lakes or swampy areas they prefer to eat plants such as water lilies, pond weeds, sedges, and eelgrass. In forested areas moose eat leaves, buds, twigs, and bark from white birch, balsam fir, willow, and aspen trees. Other plants eaten by moose include honeysuckle flowers and cranberry bushes. Moose will eat almost any type of plant food!

Moose
FUNFACT:

Moose can reach and feed on plants 10 feet (3.05 meters) above the ground. That's the height of a basketball hoop.

It is rare for two bulls to bed down this close to each other.
They usually prefer to be alone.

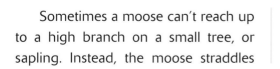

Sometimes a moose can't reach up to a high branch on a small tree, or sapling. Instead, the moose straddles the tree and slowly walks forward. This bends the tree down so the moose can eat the hard-to-reach buds and leaves.

A moose only has incisors, or middle teeth, on its bottom jaw. This means it must use its tongue against the roof of its mouth to strip or tear the food off the plant rather than biting it off. Eating this way causes the branches and stems to look ragged. Moose do have back teeth on the upper and lower jaws for grinding the food. They are called molars.

Scientists have estimated that moose may eat as many as 57 different kinds of trees, shrubs, and plants.

In winter, moose must often paw the ground with their sharp hooves to find vegetation under the snow.

Moose must have the right kind of stomach to digest their food. Like cattle, moose are cud chewers. After they eat, they often find a quiet place to rest and bring their food back up to chew it again. After moose swallow their cud for the last time, it moves into a different chamber of the stomach to finish digesting.

Because of their large size, full-grown moose need to eat about 45 pounds (20 kilograms) of food each day. If the food is not very nutritious, like tree bark, they may need to eat even more. People eat only about 3 pounds (1 kilogram) of food each day.

On most days, a moose wakes up just before dawn. It usually feeds until the middle of the morning. Then, it lies down at the edge of a field or meadow in its safe and hidden bedding area. Here it can rest and listen for any predators that might be nearby. After four or five hours, it gets up and feeds until dark. Then, it lies down again in its bed for the night. Moose are diurnal (die-YER-nul), meaning that they are mostly active during the day.

Moose
FUNFACT:

Antlers that have fallen to the ground are often eaten for their calcium by mice.

Pages 78-79: A young female moose often chooses a home range near her mother. But a young male usually travels far away to find his own home range.

In the summer months, moose spend a lot of time in ponds or lakes. Two good reasons are to cool off and to escape biting flies in the forest. Another reason is to eat any water plants that are available.

In fact, a moose may spend an entire day grazing on plants that grow in the shallow water. Or, a moose can dive below the surface—even to a depth of 20 feet (6.1 meters)—to find other tasty pond weeds to eat.

Using special valves in its nostrils, a moose can close its nose. It can then stay underwater for up to 60 seconds while it feeds.

A moose is a very strong swimmer. It often chooses to swim across a lake rather than walk around it. And it can easily swim into deeper water to find pond weeds. A moose can also use the water to escape predators.

With its powerful legs a moose can swim along at a speed of about 6 mph (9 kph). That's faster than in many human swimming races! Even more amazing is the fact that moose have been observed swimming for distances of up to 12 miles (19 kilometers) without stopping.

Moose
FUNFACT:

The moose is the official state animal of Maine. It can also be found on stamps in Sweden and on coins in Canada.

In the spring when antlers are just beginning to grow, they look like big bumps on the moose's forehead.

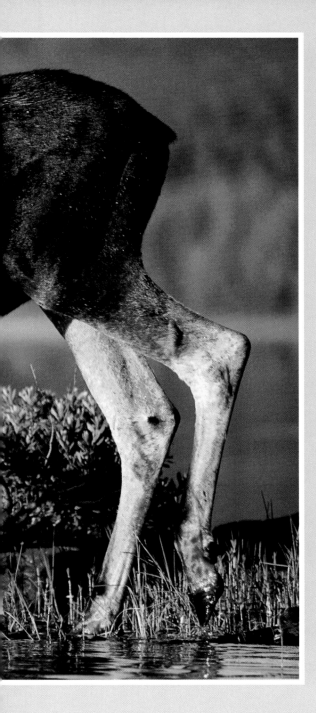

Moose have two very good senses. Their very large ears help moose have good hearing. In fact, a moose could hear a human voice more than a mile away. And with such a big nose, the moose's sense of smell is excellent. Their eyesight isn't as good. But since their eyes are on the sides of their head they can see objects all around them.

If you live in the north you may have seen a moose or two. If not, you can always check the ground for signs of moose. One of the first things to look for is moose tracks. They look like two teardrops side by side. Each track is about 6 inches (15 centimeters) long and 4 inches (11 centimeters) wide. The narrow, sharper end of each track points in the direction the moose was traveling.

The front hooves on a moose are longer than the back ones. The hooves of bulls are longer than those of cows. Scientists have learned that moose usually walk on the tips of their toes. This helps them be quiet while moving through the forest.

When locating moose, you can also look for moose droppings, called scat. Moose droppings are brown and shaped like very large grapes. They are usually in clusters of about twenty-five. In the winter, a moose's droppings are dry and odorless. That's because it mostly eats woody twigs and bark, called browse (BROWZ). In the summer, when a moose eats softer and fresher plants, its droppings are softer and have a slight odor.

This pile of fresh scat is a good clue that a moose was recently in the area.
Nearby tracks could show which way it was traveling.

These two bulls are sparring to test each other. One has already lost most of its antler velvet.

If you see moose antlers, you are sure to remember them!

Antlers are made mostly of calcium, and only male moose grow them. Antlers can weigh from about 60 to 85 pounds (27 to 39 kilograms). An average set grows to be approximately 50 inches (127 centimeters) wide. The widest set on record belongs to an Alaskan moose that had antlers 77 inches (186 centimeters) wide.

Because a moose is so tall, the top of its antlers might be over 8 feet (2.5 meters) above the ground.

Antler growth begins in early April. Two tiny antler buds begin to form on the moose's head between its eyes and ears. As the antlers grow, they receive nourishment from a covering of soft, fuzzy skin called velvet.

Antlers continue to grow throughout the spring and summer months. By the middle of August, the antlers are fully grown. It is then that they begin to ossify, or harden. Usually by late August or early September the velvet starts to dry and peels off the antlers. It is during this time that you see moose rubbing their antlers against bushes and trees to scrape off any remaining velvet. When the growth process is completed in late September a moose's antlers are whitish, smooth, and shiny.

Just as no two people have the same set of fingerprints, no two sets of antlers are exactly alike. In fact, one of the ways zoologists can identify an individual moose is by the shape and size of its antlers. Each moose may have a different number of tines, or points, on its antlers. Some are tall and thin, while others are short and wide.

Moose
FUNFACT:

One town in Alaska has a celebration called The Moose Dropping Festival, where you may see many things made out of moose scat—even a necklace!

The bigger the diameter of the antler near the head, the older the moose.
This is an old bull, spreading its legs to reach the water.

Sometimes the antlers are bloody when the velvet
comes off, but it doesn't hurt the moose.

The size of the antlers may also indicate the age of a moose. Young bulls begin growing antlers in their first year. This first set is only about 6 to 10 inches (15 to 25 centimeters) long. The following year the antlers grow larger and develop more tines on each side.

The growth process continues every year until the moose is about six years old. Then the antlers are at their full size.

Bulls cast, or shed, their antlers once a year in November or December. Sometimes they drop off together and sometimes they drop off one at a time. Usually both antlers have fallen within a few hours of each other. It doesn't hurt the bull, and new ones begin to grow in the spring.

Most of the time, moose are very quiet animals. They make very few noises. Usually, when a moose makes a sound it is because the moose is in trouble, scared, or injured. At those times, the sound is like high-pitched dog barking. Baby moose call to their mothers by whining like a frightened puppy or bleating like a sheep.

Moose also call to each other during the mating season, called the rut. Cows call with a long, quivering moan that ends in a sound like a cough, "moo-agh!" Then, the bull answers her with a deep, coarse grunt or loud bellow. These sounds often echo across the landscape for long distances. The sound of several males and females calling back and forth to each other makes lots of noise!

Early fall means the start of the rut. During this time of year, adult bulls often challenge each other for the right to mate with a cow. Two bulls may charge each other to prove which one is the strongest. They push and shove until one surrenders and gallops away. Sometimes, when their antlers jam together, the tips may be broken off or the moose may be injured.

The winner of the shoving contest is the one that gets to mate with the female. Most bulls become interested in one cow at a time. But in Alaska, bulls often gather a group of about ten cows, called a harem. The bull stays and mates with these females for about ten days before he moves on to gather another group.

Moose
FUNFACT:

People often enter contests to find out who can best imitate a bull's bellow.

This is called a "lipcurl." It helps the bull find a cow for mating during the rut.

Newborn calves rely on their mother's milk for their first four months.
Then they begin to learn which plant foods are good to eat.

The cow chooses a safe and hidden place for her calf to be born. It is usually away from any other moose. Most calves are born in May or June. They have a reddish-brown coat and dark rings around the eyes. A newborn moose weighs about 25 pounds (11.4 kilograms). A calf can usually stand and walk a day or two later. In a few more days, it can even swim.

A moose calf grows fast! For the first few months it may gain as much as 5 pounds (2.25 kilograms) every day. By the time it is one year old, it weighs about 500 pounds (225 kilograms).

A moose calf stays with its mother through the first winter and into the following spring. During this time the mother and calf stay close together. Most of the time, they are only a few yards or meters apart. The mother teaches the calf where to find food and how to avoid predators. Then, she chases the young moose away. When a baby moose is just one year old, it goes out into the world on its own.

If a moose is able to survive the first 2 years of its life, it usually lives to be about 10 years old. Some may live to be 20 years old. Their northern habitat is often harsh and dangerous, but these strange-looking animals have learned to survive very well.

Moose
FUNFACT:

When a calf is one year old, it is called a yearling.

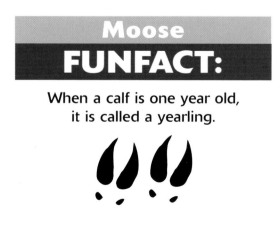

My FOREST ANIMAL Adventures

The date of my adventure: _____

The people who came with me: _____

_____

Where I went: _____

What forest animals I saw:

_____   _____

_____   _____

_____   _____

_____   _____

The date of my adventure: _____

The people who came with me: _____

_____

Where I went: _____

What forest animals I saw:

_____   _____

_____   _____

_____   _____

_____   _____

My FOREST ANIMAL Adventures

The date of my adventure: _____

The people who came with me: _____

_____

Where I went: _____

What forest animals I saw:

_____   _____

_____   _____

_____   _____

_____   _____

The date of my adventure: _____

The people who came with me: _____

_____

Where I went: _____

What forest animals I saw:

_____   _____

_____   _____

_____   _____

_____   _____

Explore the Fascinating World of . . .

Whitetail Deer

Laura Evert
Illustrations by John F. McGee

THERE ARE AT LEAST 25 million whitetail deer in North America. And if you see one, you know how it got its name!

They can be found in all of the United States except Alaska and Hawaii. They are also found in six Canadian provinces, Mexico, Central America, and even as far south as Peru in South America.

Deer live almost everywhere in almost any habitat. A habitat is a specific place in the environment where animals (and people) can live. Swamps, meadows, prairies, woodlands, forests, and even cities and farmlands are all habitats where deer can be found. The best habitats for whitetails are the ones that provide them with three things: good cover, food, and water.

The large size of these antlers help tell that this is an older deer.

It is not unusual for mature, healthy whitetails to have twin babies.

Each deer spends almost all of its life in one specific area. This area is called its home range. A female's home range is about 1 square mile (2.6 square kilometers) in size. It also must have a good place to have babies and keep them hidden from predators. Males usually have bigger home ranges.

The edges of forests and woodlands are the best places for deer to live. There are plenty of trees and bushes for cover and there is usually a good water source nearby.

Streams, rivers, ponds, swamps, and lakes are all good water sources. Some deer, though, don't need to drink much water because they get enough in the food they eat.

Whitetail Deer
FUNFACT:

Biologists often use
the deer's scientific name,
Odocoileus virginianus.

In addition to drinking the water, whitetails walk
and swim in lakes and ponds to escape biting insects.

The plants and trees that are found in these areas provide the best food for deer. Deer are herbivores (HERB-uh-vorz), or plant-eating animals. They like to eat thick grasses, mosses, clover, juicy leaves, nuts, and especially fruit and berries like apples, blackberries, raspberries, and blueberries. They also eat the leaves of dogwood, aspen, and oak trees. These foods give the deer both nutrition and moisture.

The type of food that whitetail deer eat depends on the region where they live. In the southeastern United States deer are fond of grapes in the summer. In the Desert Southwest, deer often eat the fruit of the prickly pear cactus. And in areas near farmlands, deer feast on corn that has

Deer do not usually eat whole plants, but only the most nutritious and tender parts such as buds, leaves, and young stems.

fallen on the ground after harvesting. They also graze on the lush grasses of the surrounding pastures.

Deer that live in urban areas (places near or in cities) sometimes make people unhappy by eating the flowers, buds, and vegetables in gardens. Flowers that deer seem to prefer are roses and violets. Carrots, potatoes, and corn are among their favorite vegetables.

When eating, deer chew their food only enough to swallow it. When they find a safe place to rest they bring the food back up for grinding.

Deer may rise up on their hind legs to reach their favorite fruit, nuts, and berries that are high off the ground.

A deer does not have incisors, or middle teeth, on its upper jaw like most other animals and people have. But it does have them on the bottom jaw. It also has back teeth, called molars, on its upper and lower jaws, for grinding the food.

A deer grasps the food with its bottom incisors and uses its tongue to push the food against the roof of its mouth while pulling it inside for a quick chew.

Eating this way causes the branches and stems of plants to look ragged, so this is a good way to tell if a deer has been eating in the garden!

Whitetail Deer
FUNFACT:

An adult deer may eat
10 pounds (over 4 kilograms)
of food per day.

Deer skull

Pages 106-107: If there is plenty of food in the area,
groups of deer may graze together in the same field.

In winter, whitetails get less moisture from the food they eat, and if the streams and lakes are frozen over, they must eat snow for their water. At this time of year, there is less food, and deer have to look harder for it.

During the colder months in the snowy northern states, deer must dig with their hooves to uncover any remaining acorns or leftover vegetables. If the snow is too deep, they may have to eat the twigs and young branches of small bushes and the bark of cedar trees. These woody foods, called browse (BROWZ), are not very nutritious.

Just like a cow, a deer has four chambers in its stomach, which helps the deer eat this great variety of food. Since deer are timid and don't like to stay in one place for very long, they eat as much food as they can before finding a safe place to digest it.

When they have found a good place to rest after eating, they bring the quickly swallowed food back up and finish chewing it. This partly digested food is called cud, and is why deer and cows are called cud chewers. After the deer swallow their cud for the last time, it moves into a different chamber of the stomach to finish digesting.

Whitetail Deer FUNFACT:

Each day, whitetails rest and sleep in a different "bed," which looks like an oval depression in the snow or leaves.

Even in the snow, deer rely on their well-used trails through the forest.
The trails lead to food and can be used as escape routes.

Deer do not have to turn their heads toward a sound to hear it better, they simply turn one or both of their ears.

The size of a deer depends on where it lives. Deer that live farther north are larger than deer that live in southern areas. This is because it takes more body heat to get through the cold winters of the North, so larger deer are more likely to survive. In the South, where temperatures are hotter, their bodies need to keep in less heat, so smaller bodies are better.

Adult male deer, called bucks, weigh about 175 pounds (79 kilograms) in the northern states and are about 6 feet long (183 centimeters) from nose to tail. Female deer, called does (DOZE), weigh about 122 pounds (55 kilograms) and are just over 4 feet (122 centimeters) long. Bucks stand about 3½ feet (107 centimeters) tall at the shoulder. Does are about 3 feet (91 centimeters) tall.

Southern deer are not usually as big. Those that live in Florida may only grow to weigh 80 pounds (36 kilograms). That's less than half the size of northern deer!

Northern whitetail deer have dark, gray-brown coats of hair in winter. Darker colors hold in the heat better. But by summertime, the northern deer have shed that coat and grown a lighter, reddish-brown one that southern deer have almost all year-round. The underside of a deer's neck and its belly are white. The underside of a deer's tail is also white.

A deer's coat is different in winter and summer by more than just the color. To prepare for winter, the deer grows a thick coat made of hairs that are hollow. It may seem hard to believe, but this helps the deer stay warm. The space inside each of the hairs is filled with air heated by the deer's body. The hair works the same way as insulation in a house does: It keeps the warm air in and the cold, wet air out.

The deer's summer coat is thinner and made of short, lightweight, solid hairs. The reddish brown color of the summer coat reflects the sunshine and keeps the deer from overheating on long, hot days. Deer go through life wearing just the right coat at the right time—warm in winter and cool in summer.

Since they are born in late spring, just when the heat of summer is starting, the color of a baby deer's coat is red-brown. Baby deer are called fawns. Scattered all over the fawn's coat are little white spots. The white spots help the fawn hide from danger. It is hard to see a fawn when it is lying on the ground because it blends in with its surroundings. This is called camouflage (KAM-uh-flaj).

Whitetail Deer
FUNFACT:

The spots on a fawn's coat usually disappear when it is about 3 months old.

The white spots on a fawn's coat help it hide among
the plants, leaves, and flowers of its habitat.

Scientists can identify deer by their antlers. Every set looks different—like human fingerprints do.

When you picture a whitetail deer in your mind, that deer probably has antlers on its head. Only bucks have antlers, which can be used to defend against predators. Wolves, coyotes, and cougars are all predators of deer. These animals hunt deer for food. Bears are also predators, and are especially dangerous to newborn fawns.

Pages 116-117: As the daylight hours begin to shorten in autumn, bucks begin to compete for does with shoving matches.

Unlike the horns on a cow, a buck's antlers are not hollow. Deer antlers are made of bone.

A buck's antlers may help him attract does. In the fall, bucks and does are ready to mate.

During this time, called the rut, bucks may use their antlers in contests with each other. They put their heads down and lock antlers while pushing back and forth. It is a contest of strength.

The buck that wins the contest is usually the strongest and healthiest. During these shoving matches, the bucks usually do not hurt each other.

The buck scrapes the ground with his hooves and leaves his scent, or odor, to attract a female. When a doe wants to mate with the buck, she finds his scrape and leaves her scent too. The buck uses her scent to help look for her. A buck may mate with up to 20 does per season.

A buck grows and sheds new antlers every year. And as the buck grows bigger each year, so do his antlers. A buck's antlers are usually the biggest they will ever be when he is 5 years old.

Bucks start to grow antlers in the spring, beginning in May or June. As the antlers grow, they are covered with a soft material called velvet. The velvet is made of nerves and blood vessels that supply nutrients to the growing antlers. The velvet dries out and falls off the hard antlers in the autumn, before the deer begin to mate. Bucks sometimes use branches to help them remove the velvet.

In the middle of winter, usually in January through March, bucks shed their antlers. Changes within the buck's body cause them to fall off. This does not hurt the buck, and in just a couple months he will start to grow a new set of antlers.

While a deer's antlers are covered with velvet, they may grow as much as one-half inch per day.

To help identify scents better, a deer wets its nose with its tongue before smelling. This helps the odor stick to the nose longer.

Besides antlers, there are other parts of a whitetail's body that make it very different from other animals. Deer have very large noses, ears, and eyes. They help the deer in many ways. Most importantly, they help the deer detect and escape predators. They also help deer communicate with each other.

The deer's sense of smell is probably its most important feature. A deer can tell if another animal is nearby and even what kind of animal it is just from its scent. Deer can also tell how old the scent is. This means that if the scent is old, the deer knows that the danger is past. But if the scent is new, the deer runs away as quickly as its legs can carry it.

Deer also use their sense of smell to find and identify each other. Each deer has its own scent, and as it walks along and stops to eat, it leaves some scent behind. Scent is left in a deer's tracks, and on branches and plants that it brushes against. It also leaves scent in its droppings, which is called scat. A deer's scat looks like small clusters of grapes, but the hard little clusters are more oval-shaped than round. And depending on what the deer ate, the scat may be different colors.

Whitetail Deer
FUNFACT:

Deer usually live 4 to 5½ years, but they may live as long as 12 years.

Scent is what a mother deer uses to find her way back to her fawns after she has left them to feed. Newborn fawns do not have scent, but she can retrace her steps by following her own scent. And a young deer finds its mother in a group of deer by memorizing her scent.

Whitetail deer also use their noses to find food. Other than sniffing for scent of the actual food, deer also try to find the scent of a trail left by other deer. If they smell a trail that other deer have used a lot, they follow it hoping to find food at the end of it.

Fawns imprint on their mother soon after birth, which means that they learn to recognize her by her smell and her sounds.

A deer's hearing is very important to its survival. Deer have large ears that are cup shaped. These big ears work almost like satellite dishes, scooping up and collecting all the sounds and transmitting them to their brains. Deer can move their ears to point in almost any direction, and each ear can move in a different direction separately from the other.

Triangulation (try-an-gu-LAY-shun) is how deer can easily figure out where a sound is coming from and how far away it is. Triangulation works this way: The deer first points both ears toward the sound. It then figures out how long it took the sound to reach one ear and then the other. The deer can then pinpoint the exact location and distance the sound came from—all in a split second!

A deer's small hooves help it run faster because there is less contact with the ground to slow it down. The hooves are also sharp, which helps the deer get good traction.

A deer's sense of sight is not as good as its hearing, but it is still remarkable. Deer have much better sight than people have when the light is low, like at dawn and dusk. That is why deer are crepuscular (krip-US-kyoo-ler), or most active in the early morning and late evening. Deer constantly search for food, and since they have to watch out for predators while they eat, it makes sense that they move about when they have an advantage over their enemies.

Whitetails can see very well in bright light. And they have a much wider field of view than people have—in fact, their view is 50 percent wider than a human's. But deer do not see colors very well, especially reds and oranges.

Deer have legs that are stronger and faster than they appear. A deer's legs are long and thin so that it can move quickly through the woods. Underbrush such as fallen logs and small shrubs are not obstacles for deer—they simply step or jump over them. When running from predators, deer use quick bursts of speed to escape. They also run in a zigzag pattern, jumping over trees and bushes again and again, hoping to slow down the shorter-legged enemy chasing them.

At the end of their graceful legs deer have narrow, sharp hooves. Each hoof is actually made up of two toes. A little farther up the back of the deer's leg are two more toes, called dew claws.

Whitetail Deer
FUNFACT:

Whitetails are related to moose, elk, caribou, and mule deer.

Deer are called perfect walkers. This means that when they walk, their back feet touch down exactly where their front feet had been. This works well for the secretive deer since they like to walk without making a noise. They know that if they manage to set their front foot down silently, the back foot will not make a sound either.

Whitetail tracks look like upside-down commas facing each other, almost like a heart shape. They are especially easy to see if they are in soft sand, mud, or snow.

A deer's tail is probably its most unique feature. Deer rely on their tails for communication with each other. A deer's tail is commonly called its flag.

Deer can tell what other deer are thinking just by looking at the position of their tails. When a deer is alarmed, it raises its tail high. Other deer that can see the white of the tail know to be ready to run away from possible danger. If it turns out to be a false alarm, the deer will swish its tail from side to side once, as if saying, "Everything's okay. No need to worry."

Whitetail Deer
FUNFACT:

Deer are strong swimmers, and sometimes use a river or lake as an escape from predators.

A doe also raises her tail when she is ready to mate. She holds it sideways to signal a buck. When a buck sees a doe with her tail held sideways, he knows that he probably will not be chased away.

Fawns learn at a young age to use their tails to communicate like the adults do. But they also wag their tails, just like a puppy does when it is happy and playful.

When the tail is lowered against the body, it usually means that no danger is present and that the deer is calm. When the tail is down, you can barely see the outline of white around it.

Sometimes deer lower their tails when fleeing, or running away, from an enemy. This way the predator does not have an easy-to-see target bobbing through the woods.

As fawns grow older and stronger, their camouflaging spots
fade and their mother teaches them to be alert for danger.

Sometimes during the rut, a buck's antlers may be damaged. The tips or points may be broken off.

Adult deer have several ways of defending themselves against enemies. They can kick with their powerful legs and sharp hooves, and bucks can use their antlers to chase off attackers. But the deer's best defense is to run away as quickly as possible. Deer have been observed running at over 40 miles (65 kilometers) per hour! Their long legs make it easy to jump over obstacles that stop other animals in their tracks—even fences.

Deer can jump over a 7-foot-high (2.1 meters) fence from a standing start. While running they can leap over an 8-foot-high (2.4 meters) fence. This makes them very hard to catch, and predators usually don't even try to catch them if there's room for the deer to run.

Mother whitetails protect their babies from predators as well as they can. When a fawn is first born, the doe carefully licks the fawn clean so it has no scent and is less likely to be found by other animals while the mother is away looking for food. She leaves the fawn in a safe hiding place, usually in a thicket of sticks or bed of leaves. Although a fawn can run, its best defense is to lie very still until the danger passes.

Whitetail Deer
FUNFACT:

The largest whitetail ever recorded lived in Minnesota and weighed 511 pounds.

If a fence is in the way, a deer may
just jump over it to feed on the other side.

If a predator finds the fawn, the mother will fiercely defend it. She may put her head down and ram the other animal, or kick it as hard as she can. But her best strategy is to raise her white tail and run away from the fawn. She hopes that the predator will see her tail as a target and run after her and away from the fawn.

When she has run a safe distance and is sure the predator is not following her, she circles back and moves her fawn to a new hiding place.

Whitetail Deer FUNFACT:

A 1-year-old buck is called a yearling, and usually grows thin spikes or forked antlers.

Newborn fawns are weak and wobbly, but they grow quickly and are soon able to walk and run.

Deer do not often call out to each other, but they do make several sounds, or vocalizations (vo-kul-ize-A-shuns), when they need to communicate.

When a deer is startled or frightened, it snorts. A snort is a quick, loud burst of air through the nose that sounds a little like a blast through a horn.

If the deer senses danger, but knows that it is not very close by, it snorts several times in a row to alert other deer. When the others hear the snort they know they have to be ready to flee. Both bucks and does snort.

Adult whitetail deer also grunt. If a doe feels that her food is being taken, for example, she lets the other deer know it by grunting. The other deer will usually move away in order to avoid a fight. A buck's grunt gets louder and longer if he feels he is being challenged.

Deer also have softer grunts and calls that they use when mating or locating one another. They do not make sounds unless they have to, however, because they do not want predators to hear them.

Fawns make the most noises. They use a soft, gentle whine when they are nursing. When a fawn can't locate its mother, it bleats, like a lamb. Usually the doe comes back to the fawn when she hears it bleat. But if she is eating and does not sense danger, she may not return right away. The bleats get louder and sound more like a cry until she returns.

When a fawn is in real danger it bawls loudly. This noise brings the doe back immediately, ready to defend her young.

Deer don't usually live together in one big group. Most does form small groups that stay close to one another. A doe group is usually led by the oldest female, or matriarch (MAY-tree-ark). Other deer in the group may be her sisters, nieces, daughters, and even granddaughters. Very young males are also allowed in this group.

The matriarch is the one who decides where the group will go to find food. The other does show her respect and allow her and her offspring to eat first. If another doe does not respect the lead doe, she might be punished with a nudge or kick.

Bucks do not usually live or travel together. They prefer to be alone, except for mating time when they are with the does.

Sometimes, when there is enough food for everyone, young males band together in bachelor (BACH-uh-ler) groups. The group usually breaks up when the rut begins and they compete with each other for the right to mate with a doe. The strongest bucks with the largest antlers usually win the battles.

After mating in the fall, does must wait until May or June for their fawns to be born. When a doe is ready to give birth she goes off alone to the place she has selected to have her baby, called the nursery area. She will chase other deer away that try to follow her. Young does usually have only one baby. Older does may have twins or even triplets.

Fawns usually weigh about 5 pounds (2.25 kilograms) when born. Within 20 minutes they are able to stand and walk! Then the mother doe leads it away from the nursery area to hide.

If a mother has more than one fawn she takes each of them to a different hiding place. This way, if a predator happens to find one of the babies, the other should be safe. And it is easier for a mother to protect her fawns one at a time.

This group of does can eat more safely,
since there are many eyes and ears on the alert for danger.

Deer living in southern areas have bigger ears.
This helps them lose extra body heat in order to stay cooler.

A fawn doubles its weight within its first 2 weeks. It drinks its mother's milk until it is about 3 months old, then it learns which foods are good to eat and where to find them. During this time, the doe usually keeps her fawns away from the other deer in her group. As autumn nears, she and her fawns rejoin the group and they graze for food together. They need to eat as much as possible to put on weight for the coming winter.

Whitetails do not hibernate in the winter like some other animals do. They spend their time searching for food and staying warm under their winter coats. Starvation in winter is the biggest threat to the deer's survival, especially in the northern states where there is deep snow and cold temperatures. During this time they move around as little as possible in order to conserve their energy.

In the spring, all the deer that survived the winter are not only older, they are wiser. They have learned how to hide from predators and where to find the best food. And they will teach these things to the new fawns as the year begins again.

My FOREST ANIMAL Adventures

The date of my adventure: _____

The people who came with me: _____

_____

Where I went: _____

What forest animals I saw:

_____   _____

_____   _____

_____   _____

_____   _____

The date of my adventure: _____

The people who came with me: _____

_____

Where I went: _____

What forest animals I saw:

_____   _____

_____   _____

_____   _____

_____   _____

My FOREST ANIMAL Adventures

The date of my adventure: _____

The people who came with me: _____

_____

Where I went: _____

What forest animals I saw:

_____   _____

_____   _____

_____   _____

_____   _____

The date of my adventure: _____

The people who came with me: _____

_____

Where I went: _____

What forest animals I saw:

_____   _____

_____   _____

_____   _____

_____   _____

Explore the Fascinating World of . . .

Wolves

Laura Evert
Illustrations by John F. McGee

DO YOU THINK dogs are related to wolves? They are! All dogs—from the smallest to the largest—are descendants of an ancient breed of wolf.

Today, wolves live in many different parts of the world. Besides the United States, wolves can also be found in Canada, Mexico, Russia, Europe, and China. There are two species (SPEE-sees), or kinds, of wolves living in North America today: gray wolves and red wolves.

When you picture a wolf in your mind, you are probably thinking of a gray wolf. Gray wolves are large with big, pointed ears and a bushy coat with long hair. But they are not always gray. They can be white, black, rusty red, tan, or even a combination of colors.

Wolves have a large brain, and scientists believe they are very intelligent.

Timber wolves of the same family may have coats of completely different colors.

Gray wolves are also known as timber wolves, tundra wolves, Arctic wolves and Mexican wolves, depending on where they live. Male gray wolves are about 6 feet (1.8 meters) long from nose to tail tip. The bushy tail itself may be 18 inches (45 centimeters) long. Adult male wolves weigh about 65 to 120 pounds (29.5 to 54 kilograms). They stand about 3 feet (91 centimeters) high at the shoulder. Females are smaller.

Most of the gray wolves in North America are called timber wolves. They can be found in many of the northern states. There are just over 9,200 wolves in the United States today. Alaska has the largest number of wolves: 7,000. Minnesota is next with 2,000 wolves. The rest live in other states including Montana, Michigan, Idaho, Washington, Wisconsin, and Wyoming. There are about 60,000 wolves throughout the provinces of Canada.

Wolves can leap great distances,
even over streams while they are running.

Wolves, like this red wolf, learn at a young age
to be alert to anything that may be prey or danger.

Red wolves are much smaller than gray wolves. In fact, with their pointed noses and smaller size, red wolves look more like coyotes. Their fur also has specks of red in it, which is how they got their name. From nose to tail tip, red wolves are about 4 feet (1.2 meters) long. They usually weigh about 60 pounds (27 kilograms).

Only a few small groups of red wolves can be found in some eastern states such as Tennessee and North Carolina.

Scientists who study animals are called zoologists (zoe-OL-uh-jists). They are closely observing timber wolves and red wolves to learn more about them.

Wolves
FUNFACT:

The scientific name for the gray wolf is *Canis lupus*; the red wolf is *Canis rufus*.

Pages 150-151: The different colors in a wolf's coat provide camouflage, or help it blend in with the surroundings.

Wolves have a rounder and wider head than their dog relatives. They have yellow-green eyes, and better eyesight than humans. Wolves have good vision, especially at night when they often hunt. They are able to detect motion from long distances.

The wolf's sense of hearing is far better than a human's. They can hear another wolf's howl from as far away as six miles!

But even a good sense of hearing is not the wolf's strongest sense. With a long, slender snout, the wolf has an excellent sense of smell. Wolves can smell other animals from over a mile away, which is at least a hundred times better than a person can smell.

A good sense of smell is very important to a wolf's survival, especially in winter. Wolves do not hibernate, or sleep through the winter, as some other animals do. They spend much of their time hunting, but only when necessary because it uses precious energy. They eat as much as possible when they can so they don't have to hunt again so soon. When wolves are not hunting, they rest to save their strength and conserve their energy.

When hunting, a wolf moves carefully and quietly, concentrating with all its senses.

Wide paws with thick fur help wolves walk across the snow without sinking too far, like snowshoes do for people.

A wolf's coat of hair keeps it warm throughout the cold winter months. In the fall, wolves grow a soft, woolly fur called an undercoat next to their skin. The undercoat holds in the heat from their body and insulates them from the cold.

On top of the undercoat are long guard hairs. These completely cover the undercoat with waterproof protection against rain or snow. In the spring, the undercoat is shed to keep the wolf cool in the warmer weather.

Another way wolves keep themselves warm is to curl up into a tight ball and wrap their long, thick tail over their nose. To protect their feet, or paws, they tuck them underneath their body.

And wolves don't mind getting snowed on—if the snow completely covers their body it adds another layer of insulation against the wind and cold!

Wolves
FUNFACT:

A wolf's winter coat can be up to 3 inches (7.6 centimeters) thick. It keeps the wolf warm in temperatures as cold as -50° Fahrenheit (-45° Centigrade).

Pages 156-157: Like dogs, wolves pant to release extra body heat, which helps them stay cool on hot summer days.

Look for these Big Books in the Our Wild World Series:

NorthWord
Minnetonka, Minnesota

WOLVES Index

A wolf's four legs are strong. They help the wolf travel long distances without becoming tired, even in snow. The front paws are about 4 inches (10 centimeters) wide and 5 inches (12.7 centimeters) long. The hind, or back, paws are smaller. Each paw has four toes and four sharp claws.

Wolves are carnivores (KAR-nuh-vorz), which means that they are meat-eating animals. For food, wolves mostly hunt animals with hooves such as deer, caribou, moose, elk, and wild sheep. These animals are called prey (PRAY), which means they are hunted for food by other animals. Since wolves are large animals, their prey must be even larger to provide enough food. Wolves usually hunt animals that are young, very old, or sick because they are easier to catch.

Adult wolves can eat as much as 20 pounds (9 kilograms) of meat at one meal! When they cannot find any large prey species, wolves eat rabbits, birds, and rodents, such as mice and voles. They also eat some plants and berries.

Wolves must drink plenty of water to keep up their energy and stay healthy.

Wolves are very social animals, which means they hunt and live in groups called packs. The members of the pack are usually related to one another. A pack is made up of five to ten wolves, but in areas where there is plenty of food, as many as twenty wolves can form a pack.

Each wolf pack has two leaders, one male and one female, called alphas. They are easy to identify in the group because they are the ones holding their head high with their ears forward. They decide where the pack lives, where they hunt, what they eat, and when they rest. Usually only the alpha wolves mate and have babies, called pups.

The alphas set the rules and make sure all the other wolves obey them.

Standing still and with its ears pointed forward, this alpha is trying to identify a sound.

Each wolf has its own place in the pack, with special responsibilities and duties. They all know what their place is according to a system called a hierarchy (HI-er-ark-ee).

Sometimes a wolf may challenge one of the alphas to try to become the new leader. They rarely fight, but they test each other's strength. Sometimes the alpha can stop the challenge with a long stare. Other times the alpha must growl and even nip at the other wolf until it backs down. When the other wolf knows it is defeated, it tucks its tail between its legs and looks at the ground. It may lie down and roll over on its back. Sometimes it may even slowly crawl over to the alpha, which is the signal for, "I've learned my lesson. I will obey!"

Returning pack members often sniff each other's nose
to tell where they have been and if they found food.

Next in line in the pack hierarchy is the beta (BAY-tuh) wolf. The beta is also considered to be a leader in the pack, but it is second in command to the alphas. The beta wolf helps the alphas with the discipline of the other wolves, especially when the alphas are not nearby. And when there are pups, it is the beta wolf that has the responsibility of babysitting while the parents hunt for food.

The lowest member of the wolf pack is called the omega (o-MAY-guh) wolf. The other wolves often chase and tease the omega. Sometimes they are mean to the omega, and it is usually the last wolf allowed to eat.

All of the wolves in between the beta and the omega are called biders (BI-derz). They have this name because they are neither the leaders nor the omega. They are simply "biding their time," waiting for their chance to become an alpha someday.

Pack members are very affectionate toward each other. They protect one another, snuggle together to keep warm, howl together, and help groom, or clean, each other. They also do most of their hunting together.

Wolves can go a very long time without eating. Sometimes bad weather prevents them from hunting, or they do not find enough prey. If there was plenty of meat in their last meal, wolves can wait to eat again for up to two weeks. And then they will eat as much as possible at one time.

When wolves eat, they consume, or ingest, bones and hair from their prey along with the meat. Although the bone pieces are sharp and jagged, they do not hurt the wolf. This is because the wolf's digestive system uses the hair to wrap around the bone pieces, allowing them to pass more easily through the wolf. Wolf droppings, called scat, are easy to identify. They look like hard, tube-shaped masses of hair.

Wolves

FUNFACT:

A wolf's sense of hearing is so good that it can hear a mouse moving underneath a thick layer of snow.

Wolves often eat with big bites and gulps,
which is how we got the phrase "hungry as a wolf."

Wolves may catch their prey in different ways. They can trot at a steady speed of about 5 miles (8 kilometers) per hour for many hours. This is usually long enough to tire most prey species, making them vulnerable to attack. Wolves are also fast runners when it comes time for the chase. They can run as fast as 35 miles (56 kilometers) per hour in short bursts.

Although some prey animals can run faster than wolves, wolves may still have the advantage because they hunt together. When they locate their prey, the wolves separate and travel in different directions until they form a wide circle around the prey. Now the prey has nowhere to run and the wolves can move closer without having to run as fast.

Wolves do not usually follow their prey into the water of a lake or river. This means that some prey animals are able to escape. Wolves may, however, catch prey that they have chased onto the ice of a frozen lake or river in the winter.

Pack members hunting together are much more successful than a wolf hunting on its own.

A pack lives and hunts in an area called its home territory. A home territory is at least 50 square miles (130 square kilometers) in size. Some can be as large as 100 square miles (260 square kilometers). Wolves protect their home territory and force out other wolves that try to trespass. There is usually an area between the territories of two packs called the buffer zone. It keeps the packs safely apart, and helps avoid fights and competition for food.

A habitat is the kind of place where animals (or people) can live. A good habitat for wolves provides plenty of food, water, and a place to raise their young. Wolves usually prefer to live in large wooded areas far away from people.

The amount of food in a habitat determines the size of a pack's territory, and the number of wolves in a pack. When there is plenty of food, a pack can have a smaller territory and more members. Sometimes, if the pack becomes very large, it may split into two packs.

But if food is scarce, some wolves are forced out of the pack to be on their own. These wolves are called loners (LO-nerz). Loners may try to join another pack because it is much easier to hunt in a group than by themselves. But other packs usually do not let loners join them, especially if food is hard to find. Sometimes several loners will form their own pack. And sometimes a male and female loner will mate, have pups, and start a pack of their own.

Wolves
FUNFACT:

In the wild, wolves live as long as 10 years.

Wolves sometimes need good balance, like this wolf
crossing a river by jumping from rock to rock.

The best place for wolves to live, hunt, and raise their pups is in a large
territory. Unfortunately, this kind of habitat is becoming scarce.

The alpha male and female usually mate and stay together for their whole lives. They mate in late winter or early spring. After mating, the alpha female looks for a place to have her pups. This place is called a den, and can be a cave or a large, hollow log. If the female cannot find a den that she likes, she might make her own. Sometimes she uses the burrow of another animal. Sometimes she digs her own den in the ground.

The den is usually located on a high point in the pack's home territory. It must be warm and dry, but close to water so the mother can drink without being away from her pups for very long. The other females in the pack help her make the den ready for the pups. Sometimes wolves use the same den year after year.

About nine weeks after mating, the female gives birth to her pups in the den while her mate stands guard outside. Wolves may have as many as ten pups at a time, but four to six is the usual number. When the pups are born they weigh about 1 pound (453 grams) and they cannot see or hear. They press against their mother for warmth. They nurse from her, drinking the milk that they need to grow strong.

Pups spend the first two weeks just sleeping and eating, then they are able to open their eyes for the first time. After three weeks, they can hear and they begin to move around the den, always staying close to their mother.

During this time, the other members of the pack bring the mother food to eat so she does not have to leave the pups. They bring the food to the entrance of the den and leave it there. They do not disturb her or the pups.

Curious young pups are not allowed to stray too far from their safe and warm den.

When pups are hungry they lick the mouth
of the adults to let them know it's time to be fed.

When the pups are about four weeks old, they are ready to go out of the den. The pack members howl with excitement when they meet the new pups for the first time. They all take turns licking and nuzzling the pups so they get to know each other. They also protect the pups from predators, or enemies, such as hawks and eagles. Each night the pups and mother go back into the den to sleep where it is safe and warm.

Even young pups howl to get attention, and to show that they are members of the pack.

When the pups are nine weeks old, their mother takes them to join the pack. They leave the den for good. It is time for the mother to hunt again with the other wolves. While the pack is away hunting, at least one wolf stays behind to take care of the pups in an area called the rendezvous (RON-day-voo) site. It is a safe place for the pups. Like the den, a wolf pack may use the same rendezvous site for many years.

Summer is a fun time for the pups. They chase each other and tease the babysitter by pulling on his tail and ears. They also play-fight with one another, which helps make them strong. It also helps them learn their places in the hierarchy of the pack.

When the pups are still very young and not able to chew well, many of the adults help them eat. The adult chews and swallows the food first, so that it is partially digested and soft. When the pup is hungry the adult brings up the food from its stomach for the pup to eat. When a young pup is very hungry it will beg for food by licking and nipping at the mouths of the adults.

When the pups are a little older, the adults bring them small prey animals, such as mice and birds, to eat. Next they bring live prey so the pups can learn how to hunt for themselves. Finally, when the pups are about one year old, they begin to hunt with the pack for their own food.

Wolves
FUNFACT:

Pups from the same litter can have coats of different colors.

Some people think wolves spend much of their time howling at the moon. While it is true that wolves do howl in the moonlight, there are many other times that they howl, and for many different reasons.

A wolf may howl to warn other wolves that they are in its territory. Wolves also howl after a successful hunt. One wolf usually starts the howl and the rest of the pack joins in. Sometimes wolves seem to howl just for the fun of it. And they usually howl very loudly. They also jump around and act very excited. Zoologists don't know why they do this, but the wolves seem to enjoy it.

Howling helps strengthen the bonds of the pack. Wolves learn to identify each pack member by the sound of its howl. Pack members communicate by howling when they are out of sight of one another. When a wolf howls, at least one member of its pack is sure to answer.

The howl of a wolf can travel great distances, letting all who hear it know that the territory has been claimed by a pack.

Wolves growl and show their teeth when challenged by other wolves and to keep lower pack members in their place.

Even at a young age the pups join in the howl with their puppy-like yips and high-pitched yowling. Some people say a wolf pack howl is like a beautiful song of the wilderness.

Wolves make sounds other than howls to communicate. These noises are called vocalizations (vo-cul-i-ZA-shunz). They bark, growl, whine, cry, and yip. Each of these sounds has a different meaning. Whimpering and whining among pack members, for example, is a sign of friendliness and affection. Wolves may make a barking sound when they are nervous, and they growl to chase away other wolves.

Wolves also communicate with their tails. Everyone knows that a dog wags its tail when it is happy. Wolves wag their tails too, for the same reason. They wag their tails when they see one another after time apart, or when their packmates return with food. They also wag their tails when the alpha wolf approaches them in a friendly way, and when the pups come out of the den for the first time.

When a wolf holds its tail straight out, it means that it is concentrating on something, like the smell of nearby prey.

Since each wolf has its own place in the pack, a wolf also uses its tail to let the others know its place in the hierarchy. For example, an alpha wolf often holds its tail high and the omega wolf may hold its tail between its legs.

Wolves
FUNFACT:

Wolves have 42 teeth. Some of them, called canine teeth, are over 1 inch (2.54 centimeters) long.

Wolves use scent, or odor, to communicate with each other, too. By leaving their scent around the edges of their territory, they let members of their pack and wolves from other packs know the boundaries. Wolf scat and urine contain scent. As a wolf travels in its territory, it leaves urine and scat to mark its territory.

Wolf tracks also contain the scent of the wolf. A wolf track has four oval-shaped toe marks and a large, upside-down heart shape where the paw pad touched the ground. At the end of the toe marks you can often see deep, round marks where the claws dug in for traction.

If the tracks are close together, the wolf was probably walking. The farther apart the tracks are, the faster the wolf was walking or running.

This wolf may be howling to let the pack know how far away it is and what direction it is traveling.

Wolf tracks usually appear in a straight line because wolves place one foot in front of the other as they walk.

These wolf pups are leaving the den for the first time,
eager to explore their new world.

Centuries ago, wolves roamed, or wandered, across much of North America in great numbers. There may have been as many as 2 million wolves at one time. But as more and more people moved across the country, wolves ran out of room to live and hunt. Some people are afraid of wolves, even though wolves prefer to stay as far away from people as possible. These things make life very difficult for wolf packs.

To help increase the number of wolf packs in North America, some wolves have been moved from places that have many wolves to places that have only a few wolves. For instance, Yellowstone National Park in Wyoming has received some new wolves. And zoologists continue to study them in their new habitat.

Wolves are fighting a battle to survive as more and more people move into their habitat. Wolves are listed as an "endangered species" everywhere in the United States except Alaska and Minnesota. Endangered means that the species is nearly extinct in its habitat. Many people are working hard to be sure there will always be wolves living and howling in the wild.

Wolves
FUNFACT:

The biggest wolf on record weighed over 225 pounds (101 kilograms).

My FOREST ANIMAL Adventures

The date of my adventure: _____

The people who came with me: _____

_____

Where I went: _____

What forest animals I saw:

_____   _____

_____   _____

_____   _____

_____   _____

The date of my adventure: _____

The people who came with me: _____

_____

Where I went: _____

What forest animals I saw:

_____   _____

_____   _____

_____   _____

_____   _____

Internet Sites

You can find out more interesting information about Black Bears, Moose, Whitetail Deer, Wolves, and lots of other wildlife by visiting these web sites.

www.kidsplanet.org	Defenders of Wildlife
http://animal.discovery.com	Discovery.com
www.enchantedlearning.com	Enchanted Learning.com
www.bearbiology.org	International Association for Bear Research and Management
www.wolf.org	The International Wolf Center
www.nationalgeographic.com/kids	National Geographic Society
www.nwf.org/kids	National Wildlife Federation
http://nature.org	The Nature Conservancy
www.bear.org	North American Bear Center
www.kidsgowild.com	Wildlife Conservation Society
www.wolfcenter.org	The Wolf Education and Research Center
www.worldwildlife.org	World Wildlife Fund

BLACK BEARS Index

MOOSE Index

WHITETAIL DEER Index